is

heretical Jewish poems and blessings

Yaakov Moshe

Ben Yehuda Press
Teaneck, New Jersey

Published by Ben Yehuda Press
122 Ayers Court #1B
Teaneck, NJ 07666

http://www.BenYehudaPress.com

Ben Yehuda Press books may be purchased for educational, business
or sales promotional use. For information, please contact:
Special Markets, Ben Yehuda Press,
122 Ayers Court #1B, Teaneck, NJ 07666
markets@BenYehudaPress.com

ISBN13 978-1-934730-65-2

16 17 18 / 10 9 8 7 6 5 4 3 2 1   20171008

Contents

Foreword by Andrew Ramer   v

Ayin   1

Yesh   21

Blessing   43

Wanting   65

Afterword by Jay Michaelson   93

Foreword

by Andrew Ramer

Imagine the shelf upon which this book might sit, and imagine its companions—for books are usually read alone— but seldom live alone. Imagine the authors of those other books who keep it company, even when it sits alone on your night table, breakfast table, desk, in your backpack, beside the toilet, waiting to be read.

Rumi, Basho, Hafiz, a volume of the Book of Psalms. A prayer book. No, several prayer books. A guide to meditation by Thich Nhat Hanh. And Neruda, Adrienne Rich, Louise Bogan come to mind, the last so unremembered and under-read. I'm reminded of one of her short poems: "At midnight tears—Run in your ears." And of course Whitman the list-maker, whose leaves keep the leaves of this book company. Plus, in several different editions and translations, the collected proverbs, advice, and sayings of your Yiddishe grandmother, even if you didn't have one. Yes, these volumes, and others, some slim and some thick, some hard and others paperbound—are the upright companions of this little book that you have just opened. For books are usually read alone, but hate to live alone.

The author of this little book of prayerful, comical, insightful poems is a rabbi, lawyer, teacher, queer activist. A man with many hats, many kipot, and none. While I don't know quite how this book emerged, this man of many hats and names has distilled for his readers (to change my image) a shelf not of books but of bottles, of healing remedies for our time.

But—why "Is" and not "Isn't?" Why "heretical poems

is

and blessings," when to this reader's mind so much faith is here, expansive faith, beyond categories, larger than this slim volume? Does its heresy come from boundary-crossing, identity-mergers, from weaving comedy into a subject that is most often thought to be serious: transformation?

This book begins with

> if you have an idea of god
> it is not god

and ends with

> God is the only lover
> whose absence is presence.
> Or so they say
> when the feeling of absence ends

Perhaps you do not use the word God. Perhaps you have come to call That which others refer to by that name: Spirit, or The Universe. Perhaps your practice leans into silence and not naming. If any or all of those describe you—you will find a home here, in this slim little volume that will sit with other volumes on a shelf, chattering away with other authors, or sipping tea with them in silence. And what do we make of the author, named for two of our great ancestors, the one with whom we went down to Egypt, Mitzraiim, The Narrow Place, and the one who led us out, who freed us. This is a little book of words that sit on open spacious pages whose white is its own kind of silence, inviting us to deepen and expand, to journey and to grow.

Some books ask nothing of us. They just give. This book both gives and asks. The author's self-questioning is an invitation. His musings are invitations. His experiences, going back in time and stepping out of it, are soulful mirrors. And his God, who

Yaakov Moshe

loves and fucks and shines in a million
stars

who is a he and a she, and more, and less, and nothing, is
addressed in heresy and in tender moving prayers. Some are
expected ("on watching a sunset") and some are unexpected
and long overdue ("on seeing a movie or watching
television"). Each blessing is another remedy, each in its
own bright-colored and sometimes utterly clear little bottle.
They are tinctures of earth and stars, of Jewish thought and
history, that wander out of it and then come back to it again,
to give you, in a time when the rifts and disconnections in
our world are so palpable, the opportunity to

> strip yourself of this separation
> fill this body
> so that there is no distance
> between heaven and the earth.

Ayin

if you have an idea of god
it is not god
god negates your idea
god is not anything you can think of except everything
god is not anywhere you can be except here
and when you are only here
you are not here

Sometimes you realize it, and sometimes you don't.

But either way, it is.

the memory of the timeless times
when everything dropped away
when even silence was too textured
a word

an open sky over fall leaves
an empty room
a turn in which the all looks back:

Because nothing conditioned lasts
you must let go of everything
if you want to see

your peak experiences are gone
the love and the calm are gone

If it wasn't always here
it wasn't
Is

Keep falling
because eventually
falling
turns
to
flight

there
is
no
ground

the silence that contains sound
the stillness that contains movement
the awareness that contains what is
the is that contains awareness

Is there any word you know
That you didn't learn from somewhere?

Is there any predilection of mind
That you don't share with everyone?

If not,
then who is this "you"
anyway?

hold me
as i forget

as the thirst
reappears

let me disrobe
and bathe in you
again
as if to purify
only the illusion
of impurity

let a sourceless glow
illuminate
the simplest of places
let wisdom
be carried
in a pocket.

gently, gently move me
to the next arena of acceptance

cradle me
or
take my hand
as if lightly touching
your own skin

Yoga for pessimists:

Relax, allow your gaze to rest, not on one particular object, but just in one place, taking in wherever you are. Feel your body. Then say, slowly:

Things haven't turned out so bad, have they?

My eyes tear
Is it because I am Awake?
Or because I have been chopping onions?

Yaakov Moshe

Don't worry about enlightenment. Try "liberation" first.

The only thing better than an open mind is an empty one.

Kicking
your own ass
is not the way
to liberation.

_____ is not a flaw in the system.

Yaakov Moshe

You can get to a place where everything is God and you feel unbounded love.
Eventually, however, you'll have to go to the bathroom.

If
there's
no
self,
what
is
there?

Yaakov Moshe

Listen:
Nothing is real.
Everything,
all of this,
is only in your head.

Except,
it isn't your head.

Yesh

Don't worry
about whether to see
or to love.

Love is truth
as seen by the heart.

wherever i go there you are

if i have enough faith i can surrender into anything

for you i curl my toes forward in rapture

in you i breathe air

there is nothing i love
but you
in your forms

and there is nothing i love
but you

get quiet,
and consider one leaf:
the veins, the cells,
the exquisite complications,
photosynthesis,
intricate beyond any human invention;
and then it changes color,
and falls.

and consider
how many leaves are on a single tree,
and how many trees in a small patch of woods,
and how many woods in a forest,
and how many forests in a world.

get the picture?

love and let go

& which do you need more of now

I go on a Buddhist retreat — and find You
I dance at a bacchanal — and find You
In my lover's eyes, in yellow leaves,
in the most secular of sciences — You!

If you are going to keep drawing me close,
please,
burn
me
up.

Get naked with your God
Hide nothing
Body, heart, mind,
Ideas, shames, desires, embarrassments

Be shameless
Defend nothing
to see
there is
nothing
to defend.

Yaakov Moshe

Rationalizations:
Meditating will bring world peace, or relieve stress, or whatever
Ritual builds community, gives shape to our... where was I?

Like Louis Armstrong sang,
What we mean is
I Love You

Or,
Can I be with You, as on a long autumn Sunday,
when we while away the hours doing nothing

There is a time for stained glass windows
to teach the light to children
and there is a time to open the windows

Yaakov Moshe

Translations

"And on that day God will be one, and God's name One"
means: One, beyond appellation, no longer a name

"I am that I am"
means: It is what it is

Yood hey vav hey
means:
The present
The eternal
The now
The One
The Is

Yotzer or u'voreh choshech
Oseh shalom u'voreh et ha kol
means: former of light
creator of darkness
cause of peace
but creator of All
and that means:
darkness is not away from you
nothing isn't
nothing is

the name beyond name is only spoken
when it is also what it is not

the peace beyond opposites
and the love beyond sames

and on that day
the name will not be a name

Yaakov Moshe

the kind of sad people I want to be with
are the kind
whose sadness is holy

i want to reduce all my manuscripts
to a soft kiss and a gaze

i don't want to write or teach another word
(least of all about "spirituality")
only a wink or nod to this unknown knowing,
only if you really want to,
only if you're thirsty
for this joy
that lives so close with sorrow
a roommate of compassion
a daughter of wisdom

i can only write
when i've chosen to forget

Yaakov Moshe

This poem is unpublishable

This poem is unpublishable
Don't repeat it to anyone

Like the most profound truths,
its words are banal

When stillness awakens:
an indescribable lightness
a ridiculous giddiness
an absurd, undignified love
that wants to dance in a way that would make people
laugh.

So, just a little prudence,
which the mystics might call
gevurah she'b'hesed,
a little restraint
in the name of love.

This poem is unpublishable
This expression is abashed
These visions are unrealistic
Their horniness embarrassing
Their ecstasy holy
Their answers only the Asker who says
Be faithful to me
Be faithful to me
And I will show you love.

Two roads diverged in a wood,
and I —
I took the one less traveled by,
and I wonder if the other one
would've gotten me into a comfortable, cozy lodge by
now.

Yaakov Moshe

The sense of the sacred is as real, and strong,
as the sense of the beautiful, or of love.

We may suppose that the sacred is to be interrogated,
as a statement of fact.

But I only mean to describe the sense.

What is it to doubt that a thing is beautiful?
Or to suspect that love is false?

My religion is not a matter of opinion
My religion is a matter of love

My spirituality does not depend on mythology
It requires only that you be moved by your myth

I don't care about the God you don't believe in
I want to know what prompts wonder in you
What form causes your mouth to gape
When are you so alive that you have only time for now
I want to know
when everything
for you
is here

I have more in common with the atheist who dances
Than with the so-called pious,
asleep.

So if you are sometimes in love with the world
then, sister, brother,
join me in this sweet caress
of the beloved
sometimes still and sometimes moving
sometimes loud and sometimes soft

If you are in love with this,
then you are the priests and priestesses
of my religion

Yaakov Moshe

i used to pray for many turns of events
that things would go how i wanted
for love
success

now in wiser moments
i pray only that i will remain
aware
of this

Holy one:
unify my desires.
Let me look at you as I look upon a lover
and look at every lover
as I look upon you.

Yaakov Moshe

wherever i go there you are

if i have enough faith i can surrender into anything

for you i curl my toes forward in rapture

in you i breathe air

there is nothing i love
but you
in your forms

and there is nothing i love
but you

Blessing

On creating new blessings

Ribbono shel olam,
as I compose blessings and prayers to you,
grant that my motive be pure;
guard me from artifice, pretense;
from the thrill of the dramatic, shocking, or reckless;
from becoming self-serving, arrogant, ashamed.
Cause my heart to incline homeward.

Yedid Nefesh

beloved of my soul
incarnate yourself
not as they say, once in two millennia,
but as i know you
like cain knew his sister
in the transgressive sanctity
of love.

strip yourself of this separation
fill this body
so that there is no distance
between heaven and the earth.

Yotzer HaAdam

for David and Dror

Former of humans,
what a conundrum are the shapes of human bodies!
Misbehaving, alluring, defying all sense.

Sitting on a train, a young man crosses his legs.
What follicle or cell, what arrangement of ligaments
is responsible for the arising of lust?

Which of the curves or lines or angles
throws all my education to the fire,
reduces me, captures me, turns me from angel to fool?

And, for that matter,
what magic of genetics, parentage, or Divine caprice
inclines me this way instead of that,
and yet more specifically — so precise are our wants —
to this hand, this clavicle,
oh dear, what is he trying to *do* with that... look?

All this is *hevel*, says the preacher, and striving after
   wind —
but then, who listens to preachers, anyway,
other than more preachers?

Time passes. Gravity wins.
Hair disappears where it is wanted,
appears where it is unwanted.
Lines creep up unseen.
One learns to eat with less abandon.
Indeed, flesh misbehaves, Former of humans!

is

Can you blame us for lasers and plastics, for
interventions in your strategies of planned
obsolescence?

(Of course,
really the body behaves quite reliably:
entropy, the laws of nature,
unfolding exactly as planned.)

Yet if the Earth Creature drives us mad,
still I celebrate the capacities to glue, adhere, join,
   intermingle;
for absurd enchantments of shoulder, breast, pelvis, leg
which have caused us so much embarrassment.

We marry under a canopy erected by their noble wills,
a home built for heart, but constructed of body;
a gift of the shapes of sames and opposites;
We sanctify love in a body of lust.

Former, you have made us out of earth and water.
We breathe wind as you did, and kindle fire.
Your forms to us are wondrous;
only when we look into another's eyes
do we blur their boundaries and melt.

On forgetting God is everywhere

Open my mouth and speak through me.

On heaven and earth there is none else.
But often these words are empty of awe.

One That Is,
grant me the grace of memory,
or shock me anew with the ordinary.

Remind me that this self is nothing more
than a collection of strands of You.
Remind me that it is You looking through these eyes
at Yourself.

If my desires, fears, anxieties are in the way,
help me to see them, and see them as
what is.

Remind me that there is only
the subatomic soup,
or the twenty two letters,
or the four elements —
that whatever map we use,
the territory is either empty

or empty of all but You.

On taking leave of my lover

"When disciples of the wise part from their wives,
supernal coupling couples with them,
so they become male and female."
　　　—Zohar 1:50a

As I take my leave of you,
lover,
I seek the shelter of Her wings,
and ask that it be the will of the Holy One
that He cleave to me as you do,
as above, so below,
as before, so after.
My skin remembers your embrace,
the weight of your body,
its motions as it breathes.

O righteous one, foundation,
remember me so I remember:
As the supernal coupling above
reminds the One of its duality,
so may these joinings below.

Wise One,
arrive in this absence with presence:
join me in the doubling of sames.

Tikkun Ha'Prati

Holy one, *ribbono shel olam,*
master of the universe:
You have created us with holy desires
for pleasure and union, to know you in this knowing,

And Holy one,
when I find myself alone with You,
and turn to the fruition of holy desires,
I ask that You remain with me,
sheltering me from shame and guilt;
remembering that it is You who flows through me,
not allowing new demons to be born,
but granting me memory and bliss.

God of my ancestors,
thank you for sages who built fences
in a time so unlike our own.
Thank you for wisdom today.

Thank you for the transitory gifts the body gives
before it expires.
I dedicate the merits of this pleasure to You.
Be with me now, joining.

Birkat HaChamah

1.

Twenty five years now,
I've arranged my life to sit next to windows,
craning, twisting plant-like to bend toward the sun,
to grab moments of basking amidst typing or thought.
I've met some of the country's fifty most influential
    rabbis,
and they somehow thrive in interior offices.
But not me — I've always needed you.

2.

Three months of Buddhist meditation,
on retreat, observing the arising and passing of things,
not allowing the mind to get carried away in thought
or exuberance —
a somewhat austere life, the Middle Way,
a compromise between delight and denial:
few pleasures indulged.
What's more, the weather was harsh, the rooms
    unheated;
each day began in the dark, under five layers of clothes.
But every day, after lunch at noon,
during the hour of rest before the next sit,
I would find twenty minutes of "sun time,"
peel off the layers, luxuriate bare arms and legs in the
hot midday sun,
feel delight in your weighty warmth.

3.

In April, seeing buds, humans up North greet spring
with anticipation —
a supposed return, a cyclical rebirth, angling toward
summer again.
But really we can't remember what it's like: long,
languorous days,
lying almost naked (or naked) on a beach,
or dangling legs over the edge of a canoe,
or lazing on a thick summer lawn,
stretched out in sunshine so abundant it's impossible to
    conceive of its lack,
utterly forgetting the months of cold winter when the
sun barely skirts the horizon.
In August, we can't recall what winter is like;
we're like immortal children who've never known
death.
But in April we've become inured to cold,
to complaining about it, to endurance;
in April we think we know the sun, but do not.

4.

Does the sun look different on its four-sabbatical
    birthday?
At best, each of us gets four:
the luckiest have one at one, another at twenty-nine,
then again at fifty-seven, and one last look at eighty-five
or thereabouts.
Personally, maybe I'm not so lucky.
In 1981, I was 10. In 2037, I'll be 66.
I doubt I'll make it to 2065,

is

but I hope the springtime will.
In any case, I'm glad I eat a lot of kale,
and didn't become a lawyer.
At times like these, irrational choices seem the wiser.

5.

Four is the Kabbalistic favorite; I should have ended
   the poem there.
But I'm not interested in fitting the sun into symbols.
The fifty most influential rabbis would've talked more
   about God.
But I am not influential.
Still, compared to the sun, neither are the fifty rabbis.
After all, if it weren't for the sun, none of us would
exist.
Can the same be said for rabbis?

On entering another's place of worship

Light which shines through forms,
Reality of many names,
as we enter this place of holiness,
grant us insight to see you,
grant us balance of mind
to love our own and another's forms
polyamorously for You.

As we uphold ancient precepts
by men scared of idolatry,
guard us from idolatry in our hearts,
which mistake form for Light.

As no form can contain you,
your vastness encompasses multitudes.
As your will is untranslatable,
your essence is beyond concept.
Remain with us, Holy One,
so we may honor our path
and You.

On anger

God, grant me patience
Remind me there is only You.

On ingesting plant medicines

Ribbono shel olam,
I ask that this gift you have given us
bring me wisdom and insight.
As I partake in it,
I aspire to do so as holy service,
coming to know and love deeply
Your ten-thousand manifestations.
Grant that I not become confused,
but retain my awareness of You
even as my self awareness dissolves.
Allow the joy of close contact with reality
to penetrate throughout my being:
grant me peace, enjoyment, pleasure, and insight.
And if this journey brings me to places of shadow,
let me hold onto my trust in you,
and not fear.
As I surrender some of my self-censoring faculties,
let not my judgment be unwise;
stay with me, Holy One, as I let go into You.
Keep me safe, and clear of heart,
and may the wonders of your creation
and the wonders of humankind
unfold in gentleness within and before me.

On being with constricted Jewish people & concepts

God of lovingkindness,
I have come across a word, a person, a thought,
among the holy tongue and people Israel,
which brings me uncertainty and pain.
All the familiar tensions arise:
separation, fear of separation,
contradiction, judgment of myself and others,
questioning, again, the path of my ancestors,
and the fruits it brings today.

Merciful One,
help me to see clearly, to judge less,
to return to your Presence,
from which springs the love
they and I are seeking.
Help me to see through
the concepts I cannot accept,
the people who do not accept me,
the illusion of ownership,
the folly of persuasion.

May the loosening of my constrictions
engender the loosening of theirs,
or not.

Yaakov Moshe

On going to a party

May it be your will, omnipresent one,
that I mingle now with You,
in your beautiful and unique disguises of humanity.

Let me give myself over to joy,
without abandoning my sight of You.

From the spaciousness of your Being,
I Am That I Am,
Let me be kind, and loving, and gentle.
Let me learn, and share, play, and expand.

Source of peace,
with you I am peaceful,
my tranquility rests like the deep, clear pond.
Enable me to maintain this ease
as I speak and smile with others.
As the energies within me rise
help me to allow them, relaxing my fears
of losing you.
For though I may forget,
I know that they and I and we together
are but You seeing Yourself
in abundantly colored mirrors,
emptiness dancing,
light refracting,
God at play.

On watching the sunset

Holy one,
thank you for your presence in the sun
loving warmth radiance color *zohar*
thank you for this infinite lattice of Being

Sun,
thank you for the drag you wear as God
the sublimations and projections
from you to Daddy to All

Brain heart mind,
thank you for dopamine and oxytocin
thank you for polymorphous perversity
ecstasy of colors in the sky
the capacity for awe

Shadow darkness night,
thank you too
for transmuting this embrace

Yaakov Moshe

On seeing a movie or watching television

Master of the universe,
I take leave, now,
of the present moment,
Your dwelling-place and abode,
to enter a world of fantasy
dreamt by women and men.

May the refreshment of soul
which I receive in this entertainment
nourish my love for You.
And may the genius of humankind
enrich my awe
at the miracle of life
and the beauty of the human adventure.

As I rest, now,
in the world of imagination,
may I remember when I emerge
that You are its true reality.
As I surrender my mindfulness of Now,
let my heart play in these forms,
and may the knowledge of You return
when they have ended.

On gathering with others

Holy One,
Voice that speaks through this tongue
Vision that sees through these eyes
Breath that breathes,
YHVH — You who are this moment,

May we see in these, our gathered friends,
Your light shining in each of us,
Your presence unfolding as each of us.
May we know one another
as You.
And may we greet them
with a lovingkindness so vast
and unbounded
that it cannot be conceived or imagined:
Yours.

Yaakov Moshe

Supplication

God help me heal my own suffering
Help me to be preposterous
To sit down, quiet down, listen up, be here, right now,
with you,
in all of this simplicity
and all of this complexity
I haven't forgotten a thing, Lord,
I just ask to remember This.

There is nothing that is a flaw in the system
everything that is, is you
and what comes from simple reflection
spontaneously
without a prompt or a design or a direction
is unbounded
completely embarrassing
unfit for polite company
love

Wanting

I don't believe in a religion of shame.
I don't want its morality,
I'm sick of its guilts,
Disgusted by don'ts and oughts.
Its regulations
Its laws
Its forbidden zones of the holy —
All are precautions of wise men,
who are not me.

I wonder
if the wiser men
and women
were the dancing ones
wild with foreign fire
naked and covered in earth —
the raving mad poet prophet priestesses
holy without boundaries
feared
and erased from history.

In my heresy I am not alone;
I glimpse, at the corners of my periphery,
a thousand lovers
who jumped off this train
and are waiting to catch me
if I only I have the daring
to fly.

I believe in an everlasting love that transcends the lines

of heresy and dogma
That is love, that is God, that is the One beyond God
I mistrust your word, "God"
I mistrust your love of your land
I mistrust your fealty to written law,
which I suspect is neurosis and fear.
I love God
without "buts"
without exception
I want to be the faithful servant
Who does not listen to the codes

There is more of God's love
in a dance-floor pulsating with sex
than in a pew-filled synagogue with people sitting idly.
There is more of God's holiness
in a beautiful menage-a-trois
than in the dutiful copulation of arranged marriage.
There is the beauty of God's foundation
in cocks, in sweat, in inspiration —
and a radiance empty from dead prayer-stalls.

I don't want to fence off territories of Divine
manifestation because their power is too great to
enclose.
I don't want to build a wall and hide behind it
As if what's imprisoned is pure.

The few who still remember
conceal themselves from view,
and even within their hidden chambers,
many merely mimic the dances of ancestors
which they learned, as if from a record,

Yaakov Moshe

with plastic footsteps placed on the floor by the Baal
  Shem.

The true saints are the sinners
The true believers are the wanderers
I am ready
to be pulled, dragged, screaming, from this collective
conspiracy, this insanity of the normal,
this deadened plain in the shadow of misconstrued
Sodoms.

Taught from birth the fear of our bodies
Taught in school to sit quietly in rows
While the greatest evil goes unnoticed,
riding in huge vehicles
over paved, raped mother earth —
cruelty, devastation, and a false sense of piety clothing
  greed.
The supposed sin of the slut pales in comparison with
the sin of the businessmen.
The eating of forbidden flesh —
how, I wonder, does it compare
with the beating of an Arab?

And the pious judgments
of those who have never fucked like a wind-spirit
And the fingers wagging from prissy, frozen dullards
With their brains rotting under and yarmulkes,
Never tasted
Never journeyed
Never blew their minds on meditation or acid
Never touched the dripping, oozing love of the Infinite
Never danced with God or Goddess

Never made love to Pan.
Even their love,
I wonder:
Is it as faded as their supposed devotion?

And yet,
and yet in the heart of so many defenders of the faith
there is indeed a spark,
there is such love and consideration and hope and
sincerity.
I love it,
but
I can no longer dwell within its shells.
I give up.
Don't look to me for answers — I haven't got any.
The only "answer" I know is dancing somewhere to
distant trance music
Getting beyond the self, erasing the self, forgetting the
self, knowing the true Self, loving the true Self —
and feeling unlimited compassion
which does not need to be told how to love
unlimited unlimited love itself
which needs no formal ethics and no morality —
a resting that is infinitely fast
and thoroughly still.

Does this happen to you,
at the appointed time for lighting the candles?
Does this happen to you,
when you're doing what you ought to,
fulfilling your obligation
of a commander who never existed
except in the inspiration of the few

Yaakov Moshe

who were then, immediately,
misunderstood?
Maybe it does.
But maybe I no longer feel it.

Don't look to me to lead you
because I don't know where I'm going.
Today, I want to run out into an invisible forest
and forget my life,
holding only my lover with me
and otherwise
dissolved.

I want to do something irrevocable.
I want a public break.
I want to give up on my dreams of being respectable.
I want to be honest in public,
and ruin my reputation.
Don't follow me.
Teach me, lead me, show me,
Bring me to somewhere new —
it's the new I crave,
it's the now I miss,
it's the here I want.

Outing God

Stop hiding
Enough war already
Enough hunting

I love you
but your energies can get filtered so much sometimes

Sadness, delusion are bad enough
But ignorance causing cruelty causing devastation.
Oy.

neither optimism
nor pessimism
is justified

god holds cancer
and love
and humiliation
and dandelions
and devastation
and compassion
and rifles
and peacefulness

At my hour of greatest joy,
I do not want too much exuberance,
because there is suffering,
and people are inflicting it
needlessly.

Yaakov Moshe

This is not only about Poland.
It is in the simplest of cruelties. Including mine!
And this is not about piety or holier-than-thou.
Just,
clarity
in the midst
of joy.
Remembering now,
as I hope to bring memory
to darkness.

This game of hide-and-seek:
you play too well.

So, yes to ecstasy
But enough already —
if you play this game much better
I don't know who or what you'll play with.

The truth is not out there
It's in here
Waiting for you to help it
Come out

"Jonathan took off the robe he was wearing and gave it to David, along with his tunic, and even his sword, his bow and his belt."
—1 Samuel 18:4

And Jonathan said:
Take off my armor,
beloved, David, smooth, harp-playing
Carry it like Patroclus did for Achilles,
Hephaestion for Alexander,
Handsome David,
whom my father seeks to instruct in the ways of love,
learn from me instead,
tenderly —
with a kiss
you will learn
to submit
to God.

You who want to rule
must learn how to be ruled
For Israel you will be a powerful ruler
dominant hero lover —
but for me you will be my boy,
receiving holding beautiful delicate,
and in this way train
for when you must yield
to the Lover.

Yaakov Moshe

Intermingling with me you will learn the dissolving of
oppositions
the relaxing of boundaries
the embodiment, the secret
To cradle you, teach you, hold you
I will be strong, then sweet
In a way that surpasses the love of women
In a way that rejects the piety of priests
In a way that nearly crushes your small bones
Until you release
Opposition
And cry

Humanifesto

I declare the end of the machine!
My Electronic Mail has been replaced
by My Electric Male
My Microsoft Outlook has been supplanted
by My New Outlook
Internet Explorer just took a back seat
to the Inner Explorer,
And my Windows are now open

I want to feel the breeze blow in
in the heart, the groin, the dancing legs, the mind,
the soul staring at the ice
dappling off the field
as spring begins to melt the snow

I declare the end of the machine!
The time of no-time is over!
Welcome to the era of Unproductivity
Welcome to the months? years? hours?
of not answering emails!
of not picking up the phone!
of not doing the to-dos!
of not getting back to you sooner!
sorry! you'll just have to wait!
career — you'll have to wait!
brokers, lawyers, web designers, bosses, friends,
students, teachers, utilities, secretaries, credit card
companies, movers, acquaintances, relatives — sorry,
you'll just have to take your time!

Yaakov Moshe

if i'm worth it, you'll stick around anyway, won't you
please?
while i rearrange the curtains
and go about making tea?

I declare the end of ASAP!
Now it is time for
As Soon As Peaceful
As Simply As Potentially-conceivable
As Salaciously as Perverted-imagination
As Slowly as Pitch
and mostly
As Soon as I Get a Chance

This is my declaration of independence
from "where are you?"
from "did you receive my email?"
from all the things i want to be but aren't
from the shame of not being those things
from the need to do them anyway
from sure, i can fit it in
from i'll take care of it myself
from i'll do it because if i don't no one will
from comparing
from anything that isn't conducive to joy, or
compassion, or love, except the bare bare bare
necessities
from sand
from shit
from the burnt-up ashes of the to do list

the to-don't list
the to-morrow list

the to-whatever list

Sorry sorry sorry
you'll just have to be patient
I have a scared little boy to nurture
He wasn't taught how to love,
he figured it out the best he could,
which was to stay safe by trusting no one.
And now he's in my arms
And I'm coaxing him out of his cocoon
And he's more important than being
the smartest kid on the block
the rich lawyer
the spiritual teacher
the successful writer
the person who makes my mommy proud
the person who isn't my dad
the person who met his potential
the person who lived life right
i'm too busy to be busy now
at least til this wears off

so i declare
my independence
from success

it's time to start wasting my time
instead of wasting my life
my phone has a permanent busy signal
i'm on a call with my heart
i still have letters by my name,
i still can pundit, deconstruct, hold space, act cool,
but now I want to be hot

because my god loves and fucks and shines in a
millions stars, he sees her trees all over the world, she
nurses his cross-dressing babies, all pretending they are
the center of the universe when the only center of God
is the circumference, and the only place that's there is
here, and this is it, and you are it and that is that, and
it's not what but how, and it's not should but must, and
it's not want but is, and it's not is but will be what i will
be will be what i will be and that is where i want to be
but somehow i enslaved myself to something i don't
want to be, with no time,
but now, i'm making the time to
touch me
hold me
and tell me i'm safe
so i can jump off the diving board
and fly
 and fly
  and fly

Things I wanted when I was younger

When I was a little boy,
I wanted everyone to respect me,
to give me my space.
I was five years old, and I wanted my own corporation.
I wanted my parents never to interrupt me,
they thought I didn't know they weren't listening,
but I knew they were just waiting for me to shut up.
I wanted to be important, to be known, to have a
reputation, to have the largest secret hide-out on my
block, to have cool clothes and toys,
even though my parents never bought me an Atari,
and so no one would come over to play with me.

When I was a little older,
when I realized that I had failed in my quest for
respect and admiration,
I wanted just to be normal,
but to blend in, to be cool enough, to say *I dun'no* in
just the right cool way.
I wanted to be more masculine,
to be athletic instead of the last-picked-kid.

As I got a little older,
I found out I wanted love. I was afraid of failure,
thought that my dick was broken because no girls
    turned me on,
never thought that the nervousness, the curiosity, the
    unthwartable
drive, all of that — never thought that was lust.

Yaakov Moshe

Don't know what I thought that was.
Desire for friendship, I think.
I didn't know what I wanted.
I pushed away one boy who loved me,
got pushed by a girl I didn't love enough,
chased after boys who would never love me,
met strange men in strange places as a substitute,
and now?

Now that I'm a little older,
I still don't know how to get what I want,
but I better know what it is.
And I don't think I'll pour out rambling words anymore,
trying as I say them to form attractive phrases
in order to dress the nakedness.

I don't know what I believe
but when I see a leaf I feel gratitude

This poem is unpublishable.
I don't want to reflect on it
and improve its form
I guess it is about the act of writing
as service

The heart says: trust what you feel
The mind says: that's how we get into trouble
But is that really true?
Or am I just ashamed of being soft?

I walk by the lake and feel thanks for the world
I want somehow to reciprocate
I am in love with the sense of owing.

And if the object of that love is in my imagination,
though it may be a delusion shared by millions,
people who didn't know about ATP
or protease inhibitors;
And if it's a simple cliché, an act of projection,
an embarrassing indiscretion,
a weakness that undermines;
Still it's not "God" exactly, not theology or myth,
thank God it's not theodicy,
It is, simply, unpublishable.

Yaakov Moshe

The fear that comes with love

I want to overprotectively dress you in a warm winter
  jacket
I want to make sure you drive carefully
I want you to call me after you take an airplane flight

All ridiculousness must be scrupulously observed

But I would never want to see you caged
We have known what it is to be silenced
We have experienced the closing of shutters
I would see you stretch and soar
It is worth the price.

skyscrapers

freud told us to see a skyscraper as
a huge projection of the phallic need to dominate
but what if the cock is a form of a skyscraper

i want to feel the eroticism
of a dandelion

i want to touch the sex drive
of an atom

i want to feel the power of the skyscraper
which is the power of the rocket and the cock
and the perfect line of hafiz's poem
and the perfect note in schubert's lieder

the way god rests in an eyebrow

don't reduce god to your libido
sorry if it upsets your masculinity
but god is larger than you are

I dare you to fall in love with me
I want to french kiss your soul
I want to feel up your ego
I want to massage your body
Until you feel the sparks
Of the radiant Presence herself
dancing on every skin-cell on your body

I don't care what you look like
old young woman man
even Republican!

I'm tired of accommodating
love to repression

The predicament of small mind
creates fear and war and devastation
Inequality greed hatred hierarchy structural
oppression
It turns forests into resources
people into human resources
Time into a resource
I wonder when it will learn
to make a resource
out of
the Source

No wonder the Buddha sits in equanimity
with only the slightest smile on his content face:

the love just barely outweighs
the catastrophe.

No wonder the Hasidim dance to music in minor keys,
As if to say:
God is everywhere, but I remember the pogrom.

The beautiful and the sad are so closely related
The sunset brings tears
With enough silence,
A small fly dying in my soup
Reminds me that while love may be stronger than
death
It is just barely.

Call it a sense of the sacred
Call it losing a sense of decorum
Call it bad poetry, but
I'm not half the jerk I thought I was.

Fear

I am afraid of humiliation
I am afraid of pain and suffering
I am afraid every enlightenment is temporary

I am afraid of embarrassment,
of saying the wrong thing — something stupid, unkind
I fear this path is a fraud, that I am a fraud
I fear sickness, old age
I fear amounting to nothing
I fear that other people are happier than I am, will
    always be happier
I am afraid this path leads nowhere, I've got it all
wrong.

I fear destruction of nature, evil ascendant: repression,
violence, cruelty

I fear loneliness
I fear ignominy
I fear failure
I fear disapproval
Of long-gone parents, or classmates, or friends, or self

Fear and hatred
For the sake of the self
But my true desire
Is to know You
In this fear
Is to see You

In this humiliation

and so
of all these fears,
hear us, grant us mercy,
grant us forgiveness, or dissolution—consummation—
grant us You

Never accomplishing, never loving, never giving, never
being, never achieving, never fulfilling, never knowing,
never winning
Help
Help
The words don't matter; only the tone:

I am afraid of embarrassment (strident)
I am afraid of embarrassment (compassionate)
I am afraid of embarrassment (fearful)
I am afraid of embarrassment (erotic)
I am afraid of embarrassment (equanimous)

Bathe me
in this holy sanctuary of fear
opening swallowing
surrounding in this moment
completely
in this moment
perfect
here
now
being
knowing
because

there is no I that is afraid
there is no I that fears
there is only
fearing
knowing
shaking
trusting
forgetting
believing

Hinei	Here
El	God
Yeshuati	Is my salvation
Evtach	I will trust
V'Lo	And not
Efchad	Fear

even if there is fear
here
it
is
always
now

God is defamed
When God is dragged through neuroses
to prop up illusions
to put off the fear.

You who have never seen God
touched God made love to God
because you were afraid or
because you couldn't find a text or
because you felt it wasn't appropriate

Can I undermine your comfort,
find you in your bed,
disturb you,
suggesting
that what you fear is in fact the source of life?

I will not have my love
called whoredom anymore.

Yaakov Moshe

You look around familiar places
as if one of those gazes will flip the switch again.

You put on the same clothes you wore when the magic
happened.

You ask and plead

You pretend to give up, but don't really.
If only you would.

You remember what it was like when it was fading,
how you said, it's okay to let it fade,
after all, I shouldn't get attached.
You forgot how cold it feels.

You build confidence that this, too, shall pass
You try to like rainy days
You try not to yearn for sunny days
Or, you try to love yearning.

It does show a certain depth of affection,
the way the longing aches.
In the West they say it's wiser to ache.
Elsewhere some say: ache, but don't take it personally.

God is the only lover
whose absence is presence.

Or so they say
when the feeling of absence ends.

Afterword

by Jay Michaelson

I am Yaakov Moshe. Moshe Yaakov ben Zalman v'Leah, to be precise, but we thought "Yaakov Moshe" sounded better.

Maybe it's more accurate to say Yaakov Moshe is a part of me. In the Kabbalah of the Ari, God is said to have five *partzufim*, five distinct divine personalities (literally, "faces") who enact all the roles of a classic dysfunctional family drama. And in Mahayana Buddhism (and Hinduism before it), bodhisattvas and avatars incarnate again and again, with different personae and different traits and roles. Are the gods suffering from multiple personality disorder? Or is there, rather, something liberating about putting on a mask, assuming a personality not that is entirely one's own, but, precisely by being partial, reflective of something deeper than autobiography?

That was my intention here. I wanted to share these quirky poems and blessings without worrying about whether it's what "Jay Michaelson" really thinks or believes or wants to sell or be known for. Yaakov Moshe is certainly a part of me. There are other parts.

I had a secular model as well, of course: the *nom de plume*. The unclassifiably great Fernando Pessoa developed three different 'heteronyms,' each with a distinctive literary style. Philip Roth, too, brought his readers into a hall of mirrors in which Zuckerman, "Philip Roth", and other alter egos seemed to strive for primacy. There are many other examples of writers with multiple personalities: Stephen King/Richard Bachman, Louisa May Alcott/ A.M. Bernard, Mark Twain/Samuel Clemens, Ernest

Hemingway/Nick Adams.

Closer to home, the electronic musician Moby has put out not-quite-Moby work under various different names. So have Paul McCartney, David Bowie, XTC, Eric Clapton, Damon Albarn, even Mylie Cyrus. Sometimes their reasons were contractual, the music business being what it is. Other times, the reason was, in contemporary parlance, branding. McCartney puts out heavy-selling pop records, not the scratchy electronica of his alter egos The Fireman or Twin Freaks. Taking on these new names allowed him to create music that "Paul McCartney" wouldn't play.

I'm no Paul McCartney, or Pete Best for that matter. But it has been liberating for all these reasons – spiritual, literary, commercial – to take a break from "Jay Michaelson" and be Yaakov Moshe instead. It's not meant to be a secret; that's why I'm writing this afterword. It's meant to be drag.

I'm grateful to Larry Yudelson at Ben Yehuda Press for agreeing to put out a book by a nonexistent person who, for reasons of his nonexistence, will have trouble doing book dates and media hits. He's a mensch.

Are these poems "heretical"? You can decide for yourself. The reason I like the word 'heresy,' in addition to having written my dissertation on the subject, is that heretics are believers without boundaries. Often they're unorthodox; sometimes they're hyper-orthodox. But they run afoul of authority because their minds, hearts, and bodies cannot be contained within the strictures and structures that someone else put into place. I'm not sure if I'm qualified to contradict myself in the style of Walt Whitman, that great queer avatar of spirit and body unchained. I might just not cohere. But his expansive capacity of spiritual imagination, channeled through my own particular passageways – that's the aspiration.

I'm not even sure these are poems, exactly; for sure, they're not designed for literary merit, whatever that means. To the extent they have an aim, it's to gesture at whatever numinous mystery sits inside of Robert Frost's circle, or at the happiness that does not depend on conditions – that quiet sense of spaciousness that emerges in what Virginia Woolf described as bare "moments of being." (Or Being, if you insist.) If one of those moments arises for you as a result of perusing this book, I'll be very happy indeed.

Thanks!

Jay Michaelson
First Day of Spring, 2017
Brooklyn, NY

More poetry from

Ben Yehuda Press

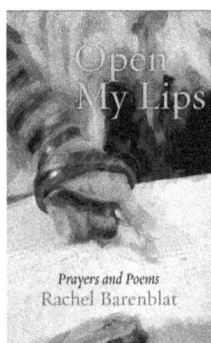

Open
My Lips

Prayers and Poems
Rachel Barenblat

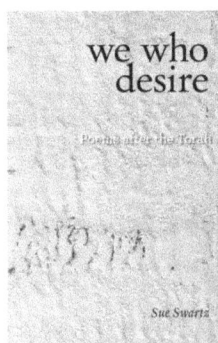

we who
desire

Poems after the Torah

Sue Swartz

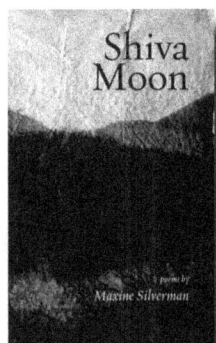

Shiva
Moon

a poem by
Maxine Silverman

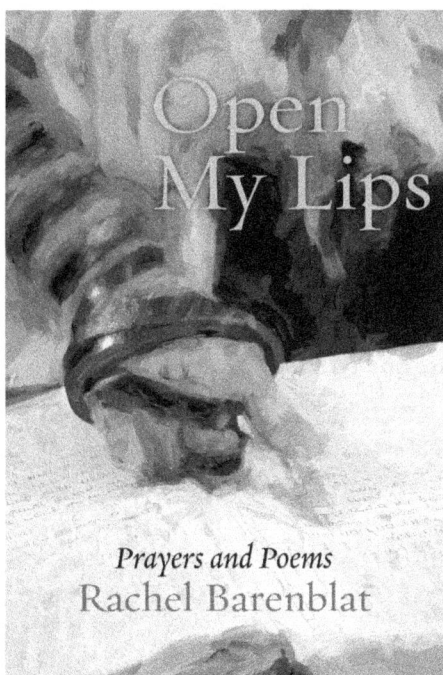

Open
My Lips

Prayers and Poems
Rachel Barenblat

"Barenblat's God is a personal God — one who lets her cry on His shoulder, and who rocks her like a colicky baby. These poems bridge the gap between the ineffable and the human. Her writing is clear and pure and the poems are exquisitely executed. This collection will bring comfort to those with a religion of their own, as well as those seeking a relationship with some kind of higher power."

—Satya Robyn, author of The Most Beautiful Thing and Thaw

Tele/Presence

I want to keep You with me
when I raise the remote
turn the dial, flick the knob

when I fall to the temptation
of reading the comments
at *Ha'aretz* or the *Post*

I want Your presence
twined around my forearm
when I snap open the Times

when I fret over trending topics
when I dream in status updates
scrolling endlessly

remind me, God, to seek You
not only in the timeless flow
of liturgy on the page

but in the stock ticker
and the commercials for windshields
and the interplay of punditry

beyond the debt ceiling
within every celebrity
there is nothing but You

Rachel Barenblat

Psalm of Wonder

I boast I grew a baby
from component cells. Big deal:

You built the cosmos
from component atoms, and those

have moving parts which shift,
performing particle or wave.

As photons yearn for the void
my heart yearns for You

though when we meet
I disappear.

When I ascend the ladder
I understand entanglement

though when I fall back down
my human brain can't grasp

the endless *ein-sof*
of Your quantum fields.

Don't go

Look how the light
is changing. Last night
we waltzed in the doorway,
sang until our voices deepened.

But our time together
is always already ending.
Weekday melodies
peek around the edges.

I'm not ready.
I throw myself at your knees.
What if even our strongest spices
aren't enough to revive me?

I know once we're apart
I'll remember how good it feels
to miss you. How everything
is meant to come and go.

Still, right now
in the light that emanates
from your face, I can imagine
how it would feel

if we didn't need distance
in order to know union
if you didn't need to leave
in order to return.

Rachel Barenblat

we who
desire

Poems and Torah riffs

בראשית

Sue Swartz

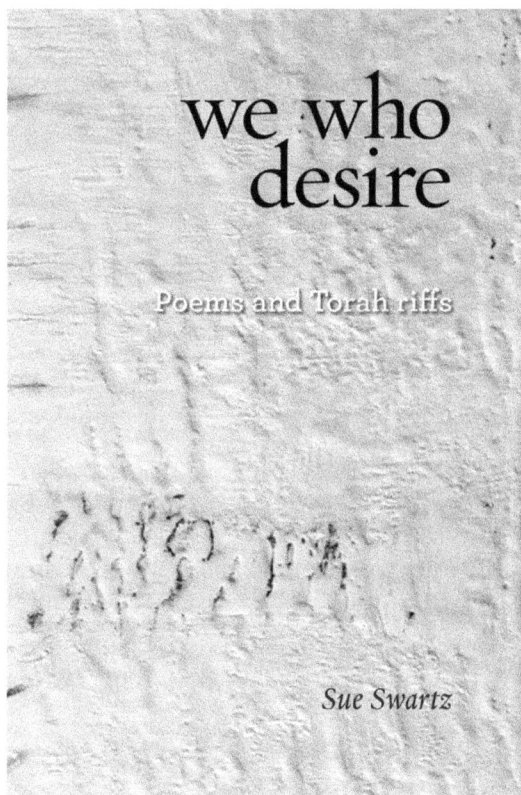

"Sue Swartz does magnificent acrobatics with the Torah in *We Who Desire*. She takes the English that's become staid and boring, and adds something that's new and strange and exciting. These are poems that leave a taste in your mouth, and you walk away from them thinking, what did I just read? Oh, yeah. It's the Bible."
—Matthue Roth, author, *Yom Kippur A Go-Go, Never Mind the Goldbergs, My First Kafka*

ELEGY

His sons Isaac and Ishmael buried him—

Everything begot then begets its opposite:
nothing stays itself for very long.

It was time for Abraham to go, and for his sons—

One sent out, hand pressed firmly on his back,
one led forward by deception luminous as the stars—

To bury him.

Oh, to be a fly on the wall at Machpelah as the grand
patriarch is laid within.

Tell me. Which son would speak first of his restless
consolations?

Which of his many little deaths?

Sue Swartz

APOLOGIA

The people stood at the foot of the mountain—

We were unbound then // awakened from watery sleep
when the earth cracked open & sound poured out like lava.

We were undecided then // bathed in sulfur and smoke
when thunder split the mountain // when lightening

scorched our heels. Poised on the edge of desire // enveloped
by rumbling flashes, the words entered our consciousness

like a tornado—
          In the bleached-blind wilderness we stood // amid
fire clouds and roaring triumph // amid searing trumpets

& our endless endless wanting // and we were afraid.
Ruthless present tense // Mobius arc of time—

We were joined to each other then // to the blistering
mountain // the vertiginous moment // every noun and verb

exploded through the wilderness. Chosen agnostics,
we declaimed yes to deliverance // yes to unspecified

constraint. To the shattering of silence // to the shattering
of stone. For you not yet able to speak, we said *yes.*

Shiva Moon

poems by
Maxine Silverman

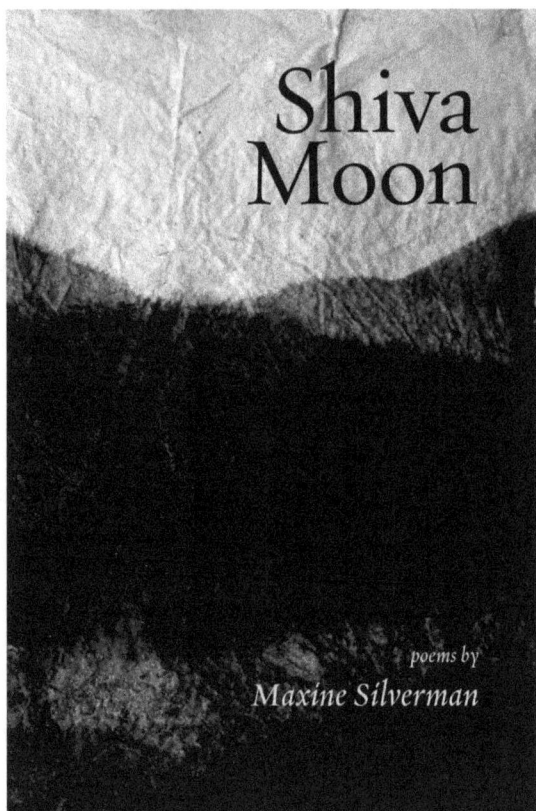

"Intimate and meditative, SHIVA MOON has the quality of prayer, yet it's also the journal of a harrowing year, filled with mourning, recollection, and a struggle for spiritual equilibrium. With her celebrated gifts for pictorial and lyrical language (leavened here with Hebrew terms), Maxine Silverman enters the darkness of her beloved father's death and seeks a way to accommodate his loss. Everything around her keeps changing: the moon, her garden, her children, even her absent father who grows more vivid with memory. The only constant is the momentous presence of God, glorious but silent. This is a wise, moving book for every reader—and a necessary book for anyone who's known loss."
—**Joan Murray**, author, *Swimming for the Ark*

Maxine Silverman

Leviticus 18:7

how else to wash the exhausted body,
to marvel at breath's tangible beauty,

to murmur psalms all night long

What I Learned So Far (5)

Umbra and penumbra,
perigee, when to plant a tree,
Kaddish deRabbanan,

Aldebaran . . . Castor, Pollux
. . . Capella

in other words, the winter hexagon,
one of those fabrications
for plumbing the fathoms of night.

Specialized bodies of knowledge,
disciplines,
require their own language,

grief's aleph bet,
the jargon of mourning,
a grammar of loss and longing
in the context of love v'kavanah.

I learned   palimpsest is richer
than irony to convey shades
of meaning,
             k'riah or any visible sign
of mourning are not worn on Sabbath,
             pentimento may explain
faces of people "not there,"
             zachor—a life's work.

Maxine Silverman

www.ingramcontent.com/pod-product-compliance
Lightning Source LLC
Chambersburg PA
CBHW031142090426
42738CB00008B/1182